'Witty subversion combined
with compelling realism'

Philip Mould OBE

Venetian Fragment (study) · oil on canvas · 11.3 x 20 cm

TRAHISON DES CLERCS

A betrayal of intellectual, artistic or moral standards by writers, academics or artists

THE TITLE IS BORROWED FROM *LA TRAHISON DES CLERCS*, JULIEN BENDA'S

ACCOUNT OF INTELLECTUAL CORRUPTION IN EUROPE IN THE 1920S

ORIGINALLY PUBLISHED IN FRANCE IN 1927

PETER GOODFELLOW

TREASON
of the SCHOLARS

PANTER & HALL

THE EXHIBITION

Treason of the Scholars

21ST OCTOBER—6TH NOVEMBER 2015

PANTER & HALL

11–12 PALL MALL, LONDON, SW1Y 5LU

TELEPHONE 020 7399 9999

ENQUIRIES@PANTERANDHALL.COM

WWW.PANTERANDHALL.COM

CONTENTS

TREASON OF THE SCHOLARS

It all began in New York in 1917, when a young French emigré, Marcel Duchamp, submitted a urinal, signed 'R. Mutt' and entitled *Fountain*, to the Society of Independent Artists annual exhibition. The piece was rejected but 'Modern Art' was born.

Or so a poll of '500 art experts' decided in the run-up to the Turner Prize in 2004. Warhol's *Marilyn Diptych* came third in the ballot; Picasso's *Les Demoiselles d'Avignon* second, while Duchamp's *Fountain* was the easy winner as 'the most influential modern art work of all'.

And on this at least–if perhaps on nothing else–the judgment of the '500 art experts' is to be believed.

But one thing is also clear. There was no 'treason'–no betrayal or bad faith or dishonesty–and certainly no 'fakery' (Roger Scruton's preferred term) about the behaviour of the Duchamp of 1917 at all. Quite the contrary. The thirty-year-old Duchamp was as open and honest about his beliefs–or non-beliefs–as any man could be. And his actions corresponded to the letter.

He was a member of a loose-knit group of artists, writers and intellectuals who called themselves 'Dada'. 'Dada' was a nonsense word for a group devoted to the subversion of reason and meaning in Art, Literature and Life. For, according to the Dadaists, unreason was the only sane response to a world made mad with the unimaginable, unprecedented horrors of the First World War which was then raging.

Duchamp was at once the most intelligent and creative of the group. He called himself an anti-artist or (on the lines of 'anarchist') an 'an-artist'. Like his fellows, he rejected comprehensively 'Art' and everything to do with it–its aesthetics, institutions and achievements. There were, he proclaimed from the roof-tops, no artists and no works of Art. No one and nothing. And what were called such had no value–and no monetary value in particular: 'Rembrandts should be used as ironing boards', he is supposed to have declared in one of his milder sayings.

Duchamp's genius (and I use the word advisedly) was to translate these vaguely Leftist verbal postures into a series of brilliant visual gestures or puns. The urinal was by far the best. It was non-art, by a non-artist (indeed by a non-person, 'R. Mutt'). It was mildly smutty (the 'Dadaists' had a schoolboy love of smut). It (the urinal, that is) was turned upside-down, like the world. And–with its elevated title 'Fountain' and its submission to an annual exhibition–it mocked perfectly the pretensions of those who thought they *were* artists and knew what Art was.

So far, so honest.

But Duchamp did not limit himself to the urinal or–to give it its term of art (!)–*objet trouvé* (found object) or 'ready-made'. He also, and in an astonishingly short period of time, came up with a whole series of other, 'non-art' forms. He created 'kinetic', that is, moving 'sculptures': some simple, like a mounted rotating bicycle-wheel; others more elaborate which produced various optical illusions when spun at speed on the turntable of a gramophone. He gave them the name 'mobiles', which, like so many of the gestures he tossed off, has stuck.

He shot films of his 'mobiles' in motion. He used graffiti to debunk and shock, painting a neat Poirot-style mustache and beard on a reproduction of the Mona Lisa. He gave fanciful and often heavily sexualised titles to his most apparently mechanical creations, like *The Bride Stripped Bare by Her Bachelors, Even*'. He made extensive use of chance, whether falling bits of string in one of his multimedia assemblages, or mechanical devices to produce a random 'musical' happening– and this last when John Cage was still in his cradle. He dressed as a woman (shades of Gayson Perry) and had himself photographed as such under the name of Rrose Sélavy. He even came up with the term 'conceptual' to describe all this–as opposed to the merely 'retinal' or eye-pleasing Art of the past.

In short, there is barely a trick in the Turner Prize book which the young Duchamp did not anticipate and then some.

But then, still only in his early thirties, he gave it all up and devoted most of the rest of his life to playing, studying and writing about chess. Had he got bored? Was he overcome by the sheer, absurd pointlessness of constantly attacking something (Art) which he professed to believe did not exist? Or, worst of all, did he already have intimations his anti-art might transmogrify–horror of horrors–into a zombie, life-after-death version of the hated Art itself?

We do not know. But, once again, there is an honesty, perhaps a sort of nobility, in Duchamp's renunciation and self-exile into the world of chess. He even, like Christ in the Wilderness, underwent temptations which–Christ-like again–he resisted, at least for a time. First to play the role of Tempter was the director of the Knoedler Gallery in New York who in the 1930s offered him a substantial sum if he would continue to produce the Cubist-like works for which he was then best known. Duchamp brushed the offer aside, declaring loftily: 'It would force me to repeat myself. I will not even envisage this possibility.' Duchamp also worried, as his 'ready-mades' became better known after the Second World War, that they might succumb to the 'aesthetics of patina' and become venerated as Art-objects themselves. Perhaps, he wondered, he should swap them

for newer mass-produced objects and replace, for example, his *Bottle Dryer* with a plastic bucket?

He never quite got round to it. But always there was the consolation of chess. 'I am still a victim of chess', he declared. 'It has all the beauty of Art–and much more. It cannot be commercialised. Chess is much purer than Art in its social position.'

Brave words. But could this self-proclaimed purity survive the full onslaught of fame and fortune in the Sixties when Duchamp was rediscovered; hailed as a cultural (or was it a *counter*-cultural) icon and recognised as the grandfather of everything from Pop Art to the happening?

At first, it seemed as though it might, as Duchamp continued to show himself not to be without honour. In 1961, when the mad, tawdry decade had barely begun, one of his fellow surviving Dadaists wrote to Duchamp, putting a pungent denunciation of the New Art into his mouth: 'This Neo-Dada', (the writer made Duchamp declare), 'which they call New Realism, Pop Art, Assemblage, etc., is an easy way out, and lives on what Dada did. When I discovered the ready-mades I sought to discourage aesthetics. In Neo-Dada they have taken my ready-mades and found aesthetic beauty in them. I threw the bottle-rack and the urinal in their faces as a challenge and now they admire them for their aesthetic beauty.'

Every word of course was true. Sixties Art–for all its self-proclaimed newness–was hopelessly old-hat and derivative. It was also, since it turned Duchamp's anti-art into Art and venerated it accordingly, morally defective. Duchamp recognised all this and scrawled his approval in the margin of the letter in his characteristic *franglais*: 'OK. ça va très bien'. It *was* a gesture of dissent. But it was not a very loud or clear one. And soon he yielded to the times. The actual moment of the Fall came in 1964. Early that year, the Art-dealer Arturo Schwarz mounted an exhibition entitled *Omaggio a Marcel Duchamp* in his gallery in Milan. The exhibition included reproductions of two of Duchamp's 'readymades' and Duchamp came to Milan for the opening.

What happened next is unclear and in dispute. Schwarz claimed that it was Duchamp who took the initiative. Concerned that many of his 'ready-mades'–including the *Fountain* itself–had been lost, he suggested that Schwarz should make an edition of thirteen of them. But why, if Duchamp's concern about the 'oblivion' of his '*oeuvre*' (oh that Bad Old Art word!) were real, was it necessary for the edition to include surviving as well as lost works? Why make eight numbered copies of each? And why sign each and everyone of them with Duchamp's real name, thus reviving at a stroke 'the fallacy of romanticizing the conscious individuality of the artist' which the young Duchamp had satirised and subverted with his female impersonation as Rrose Sélavy?

The safest assumption is that Schwarz was lying and that the idea of the edition was his from the beginning. But, by listening to this new Mephistopheles and going along with his scheme, Duchamp threw away his integrity, which he had guarded so long, and embraced bad faith.

In his seventies he had become what in his youth he had most despised: an Artist.

What is worse–and is the real 'treason'–is the way in which Duchamp tried to justify himself. In 1967, with barely sixteen months to live and in what amounted to his valedictory inter-view ('Quite simply, I am waiting for death', he declared), he was confronted with the 'paradox'. How, his interviewer asked, could he justify that his 'ready-mades' had 'ended up being 'consumed' in museums and exhibitions, and sold as art objects'? And why had he exacerbated the process by acquiesc-ing in the multi-copy signed editions of the Galleria Schwarz? 'There is an absolute contradiction', Duchamp conceded. 'But that is what is enjoyable, isn't it?', he added quickly. 'Bringing in the idea of contradiction . . . which is something that has

never really been used, you see'. This is shameless. By wriggling on a word, Duchamp was trying to have his cake and eat it.

In so doing, Duchamp completed his Fall. He was no longer merely a mercenary Artist. He had become a Fake and a pur-veyor of Fakes–each numbered, signed and priced as with the triple Mark of the Beast.

Strikingly, the moral case against Duchamp turns on a word: 'contradiction'. Which takes us back to the beginnings of Dada itself. For Dada was not only an attack on Art but on Literature and Language as well:

> I shall be reading poems that are meant to dispense with conventional language, (Hugo Ball declared in the first *Dada Manifesto* of 1916). I don't want words that other people have invented . . . I want my own stuff . . . a chance to get rid of all the filth that clings to this accursed language as if put there by stockbrokers' hands, hands worn smooth by coins.

Stirring stuff, even if the example given–'Dada Tzara, . . . dada m'dada, dada m'dada dada mhm'–is perhaps less than compelling. But there is a problem, which is tackled with un-Dada-like economy by Lewis Carroll in Alice's encounter with Humpty-Dumpty.

For Humpty-Dumpty too had a way with language. 'When I use a word', Humpty-Dumpty said, in a rather scornful tone, 'it means just what I want it to mean– neither more nor less'. 'The question is', said Alice, 'whether you can make words mean so many different things'. 'The question is', said Humpty-Dumpty, 'which is to be master–that's all'.

'Which is to be master–that's all'. In other words, changing language is about changing power. Each revolution, as George Orwell understood so clearly, tries to invent a New Speak to impose its view of the world. Neo-Dada–following as ever in the footsteps of Dada–has been extraordinarily successful

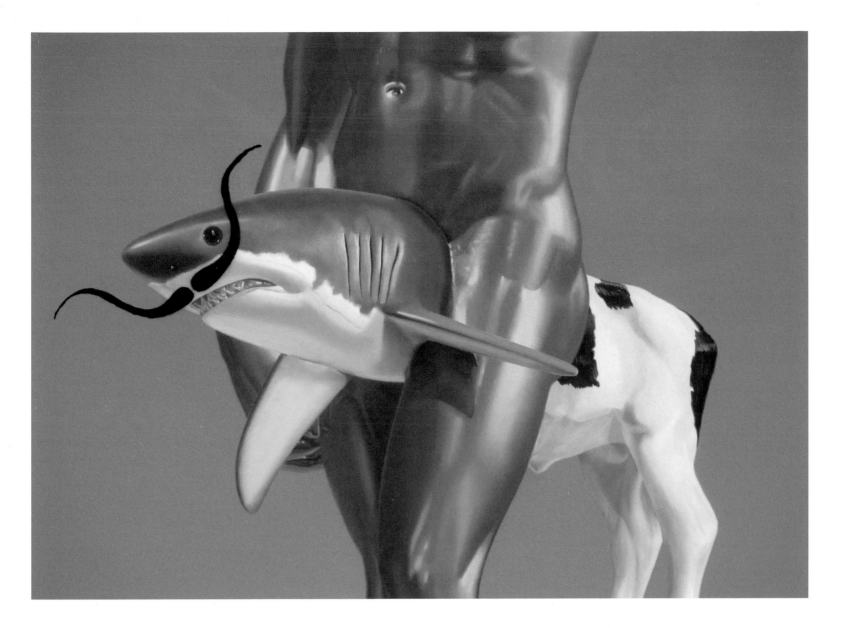

in this endeavour. All discrimination and all concerns about petty things like contradiction have been washed away in a slew of nonsense words: 'Dada Turner Prize. Dada m'dada MOMA. Dada Pompidou. Dada m'dada Money'.

But there is nothing nonsensical about the result, which can now be seen every year in the pomp and circumstance of Royal Academy Dinner. It is a scene worthy of Orwell's savage pen; indeed it takes only the lightest alteration to make him describe it:

The guests looked from Young British Artist to Royal Academician, and from Royal Academician to Young British Artist, and from Young British Artist to Royal Academician again: but already it was impossible to say which was which.

How Duchamp, at least the rotten old one, would have giggled appreciatively at the 'absolute contradiction'!

David Starkey

CONCEPTUAL ART

Art in which the idea presented
by the artist is considered
more important than the
finished product

ART

*The expression or application
of creative skill and imagination,
especially through a visual
medium such as painting
or sculpture*

Brave New World (Baby Peter, Mickey and Jeff) · oil on linen · 70 x 150 cm

DECLINE AND FALL

It was dark, 11.30 at night, December 17th 2009, and I had just landed at Venice airport in time to catch the last bus to the city. Arriving at the terminal it was a Vaporetto to the lagoon and a cheap hotel near St. Mark's square. I was full of excited anticipation for what awaited me at dawn.

I was there for four days, to walk the streets. This quiet time of year was perfect as I would avoid the tourists the Carnival and the Biennale. No holiday this but a research trip. Like many artists before me I was there to absorb the visual stimulation of what has to be the finest example of urban landscape in Western civilisation.

I was lucky, temperatures of minus one and clear blue skies meant that the milky green colour of the water, so rare in nature, confirmed that all those Canalettos do not lie, and La Serenissima did not disappoint as I was overloaded with fascinating shapes, textures, colours and compositions. For a painter it was like a child in a sweetie shop, even the scruffy seediness of the back alleys had their treats, but this aspect of the city started me thinking about what needs doing, what needs saving, what needs spending money on and how come this great example of the glory of human achievement hosts the Biennale? It is the antithesis of all that is spectacular about the city, with its trite, pretentious, ugly installations and meaningless platitudes that justify it all. There is no shortage of money here.

The seed for this exhibition was sown right then; for I was angry. Angry and embarrassed at what our visual arts culture has become. Think about who we choose to represent Britain at such prestigious showcases. Not a gifted painter or sculptor

in sight. No ability, no technique, no intellectual gravitas. Unadulterated hubris and self-indulgence.

I had finally woken up to the realisation that my passion, my culture, my industry had been hijacked by greedy charlatans and pseudo intellectuals who now controlled the upper echelons of our cultural life. They have also managed to suppress criticism from many quarters. Politicians have not the wit to question their actions as they shy away from anything associated with the visual feigning a lack of understanding, or ignorance. It reminds me of FIFA and the administrators of the NHS, vested interests and a protected market that cannot be allowed to fail. There is too much money involved.

Unmade beds, a glass of water that is (apparently) an oak tree, rotten meat, the murder of creatures for art (my *Treason of the Sheep Skull* died naturally), light bulbs going on and off, badly edited little films, vacuous soundscapes.

I have come to the conclusion that the cult of self is largely to blame, and the beatification of curators who used to do their jobs in a scholarly and unassuming way and now crave celebrity status as much as the brand artists they thrust upon us ad infinitum.

'*I am an artist*' ergo, anything I do is art. One of the advantages of this bogus philosophy is that a relatively easy and lazy existence lies ahead. You do not have to manifest *any* semblance of the abilities and skills that were once prerequisite.

We have dropped our allegiance to the Greco–Roman visual tradition which has held sway over our culture for

Decline and fall of Western civilization (detail)

two millennia. It is what has marked out our unique Western interpretation of looking at things and is entirely different for example from Japanese ways of seeing.

I am an artist, categorically and fundamentally. But the only art I make is when I paint, draw, or occasionally sculpt. At other times I may be a cook or a mountain biker, but I am not an artist then. I am not making art when I go for a walk. I may create a painting from something I saw on the journey but the walk itself is not art. I may stop and make or leave something in the landscape whilst I am out walking and that may or may not be art. The act of motion is not art. Neither is the motion I leave in the bathroom.

Nowadays artists *practice*.

I do not practice. I squeeze oil paint from tubes and apply this with brushes or palette knives to wood or canvas. The result is a painting. I paint.

As Duncan Macmillan says,
> At one Art College, at least, perhaps at many others, Sculpture has become Contemporary Art Practice. This is a piece of International Art English obfuscation institutionalised. As it is not fashionable to make art, some other word must be found to describe the activity and 'practice' is now cant for what artists do. But doctors practice, dentists practice, so do lawyers–so do Christians for that matter. The word means to profess and the point of this usage among professionals is that they deploy their skills in the service of others. When they stop serving others they no longer practice. There is no suggestion that artists are now more than ever before working in the service of others, on the contrary, acute solipsism is a common feature of the work of most of those who are fashionably contemporary.

There are many artists who do what I do, a lot of them extremely well. But you would not know of them; they have been ignored by all the regional and national curators for three decades and they receive no support from any of our arts institutions. Traditional skills are no longer pursued at Art College. Students are encouraged to have 'concepts'.

Three tendencies can lead to success: Gigantism, Casting and Bling.

In the first instance you take a form or everyday object, however uninteresting it might be, and make it enormous.

In the second instance, take any organic body part or manufactured product and cast it in some other material. In the case of metal this will render it impossible to lift, thus attracting a weighty intellectualism.

Finally use gold, diamonds, or other expensive raw materials and any insignificant piece acquires reverential status.

As useful as these tricks are, the trump card is waiting in the wings. Having avoided traditional skills because of a lack of ability in them in the first place, the brand artist will return to them like the prodigal son.

Embraced by a host of compliant and sycophantic curators their drawings and paintings will be hung next to venerable dead masters, in the delusional belief that hanging by association will elevate their poor attempts at these disciplines.

What is truly astonishing is that nobody is remotely ashamed or embarrassed by this visual vandalism neither artist nor curator, nor for that matter the custodian Director of the Museum who has facilitated the charade.

Legacy of Joseph Beuys (detail)

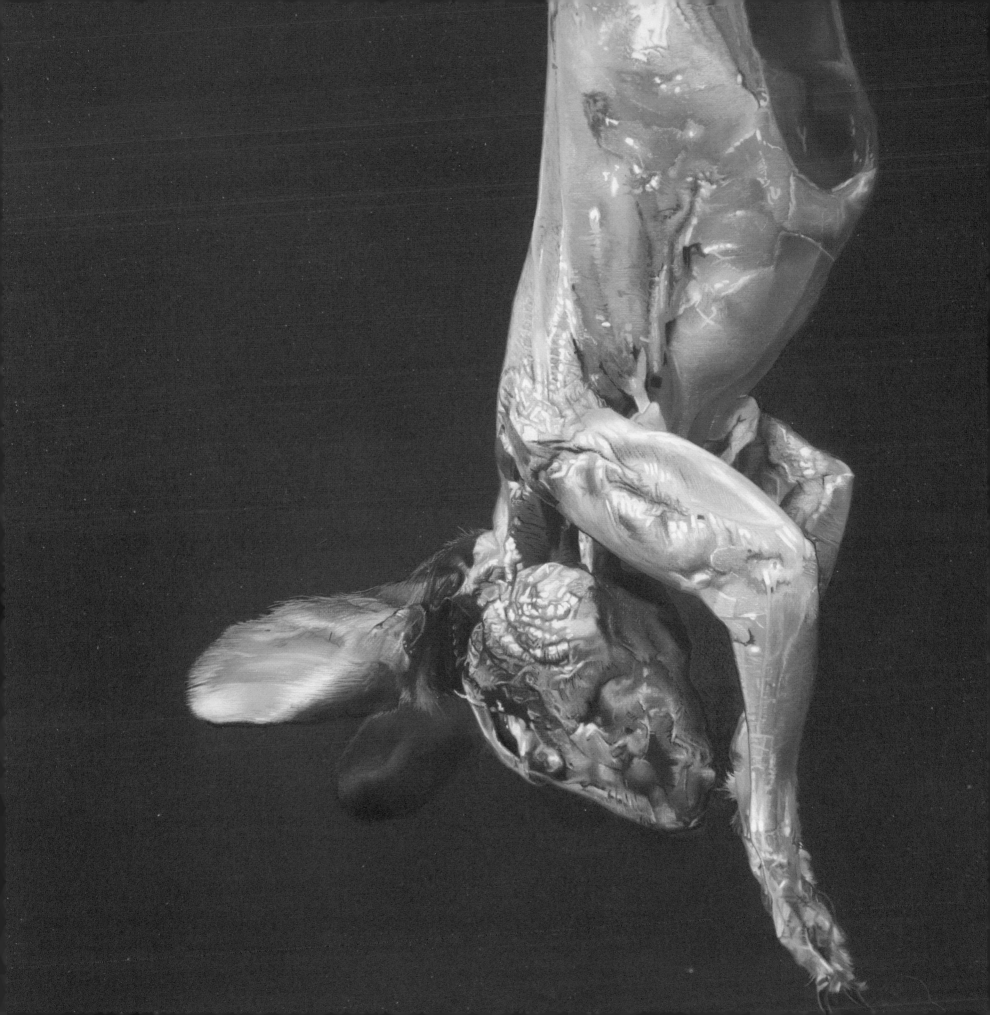

In Britain we have the Turner Prize which is second only to the Venice Biennale in international status. For the last 20 years most of the nominees and winners have been conceptualists, film makers, window dressers, and occasionally bad painters. In 2014 there was even a clipboard accompanied by a market researcher.

With the exception of Grayson Perry, they all lack the ability and perception of a true artist. I suspect it was his transvestism that alerted the Turner Quango rather than his highly original take on the ceramicist's art.

Indeed it seems to me that a singular lack of ability is essential to gain entry to the Turner Prize Club. However, it opens up big possibilities for them post-competition as museums and cultural events fawn all over them to participate in activities which are seemingly unrelated to anything they evidenced in their submissions on show at the Tate.

So, if you would like a tail fin design for a jumbo jet, or a play for the theatre, or an Olympic poster, ask a Turner Prize entrant. Never mind that a graphic designer or playwright would do a much better job.

More erudite writers in this book will cast a brighter light on this travesty, but I hope my paintings will enlighten a bit more than words alone.

Peter Goodfellow

The Two empty vessels (detail)

abandon abominable absurd
abysmal acquiesce adherent
ad-nauseum adulation anathema
apologist **apostasy** arriviste
arrogant artifice artificial avarice

Madonna of the Kitsch · mixed media · 55 x 27 x 10 cm

23

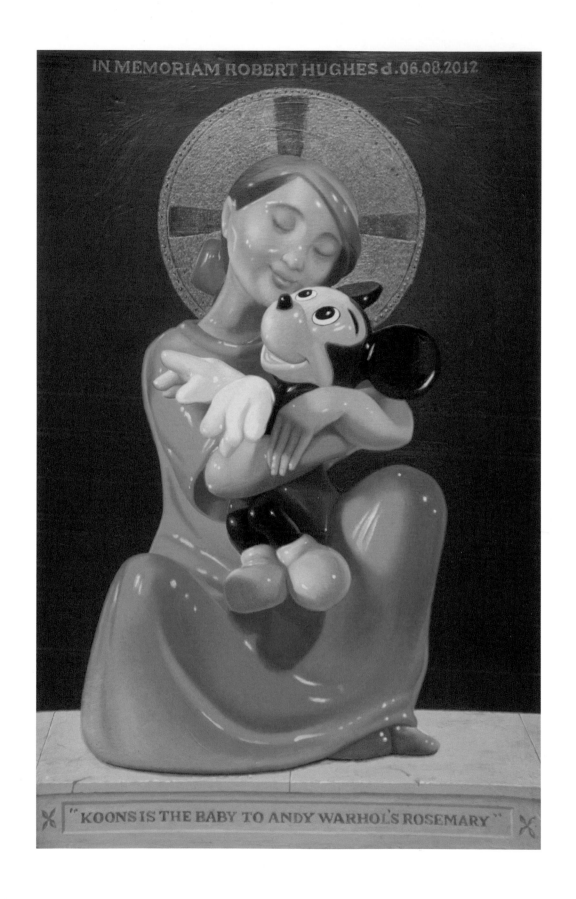

balderdash bamboozle
banal bandwagon
barefaced barren base
betrayal bias blatant
boastful bogus bombast
brainwash brand brazen

The Decline and Fall of Western Civilization · oil on canvas · 120 x 150 cm

XIV

RVTLI
e
UCLET

Me

Me

Me

TAE EI
2007

972

cabal
carrion
casuist
charade
charlatan
claptrap
clique
coerce
collusion
complicit
condone
connive
corruption
coterie
credulous
cronyism
curator

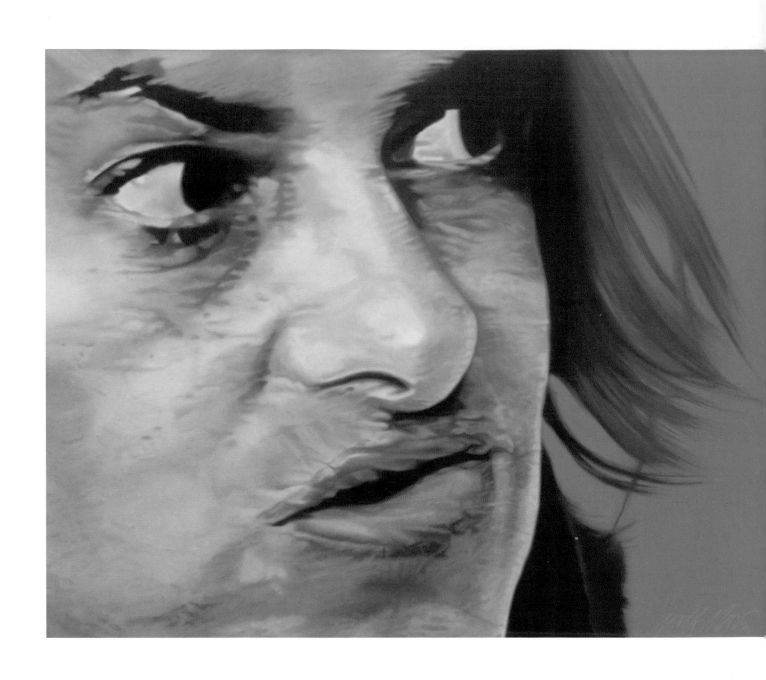

The Gaze of Narcissus · oil on linen · 70 x 210 cm

Cup Cake Montserrat · oil on linen · 46 x 41 cm

Cup Cake Tracey · oil on linen · 46 x 41 cm

THE THOUGHT POLICE

Thought Police A group of people who aim to suppress ideas that deviate from the way of thinking that they believe to be correct.

Since the Renaissance, the evolution of the West has hinged on one key idea: we can only understand the world by observing and describing it as truthfully as we can. If that is so, there is one skill above all that has enabled us to do this: drawing. It is no accident that the Renaissance had drawing at its heart. Nor was its usefulness limited to the arts. Science as it became known depended as much as art on drawing's unique ability to record and analyse and so provide a route to understanding whatever the inquirer observed. Advances in medicine would have been impossible without drawing to record, illuminate, and also to publish and so share, the observations of anatomists and surgeons. That is just as true of the other sciences, while advances in engineering and technology would have been unthinkable without the skill that makes it possible to project and test ideas, to guide their implementation and to make calculations visible. How ironic then that the last few decades that have seen the rapid decline of the West's hegemony should also be the decades in which drawing, so important in so many ways and the basis of all art teaching since the Renaissance, should be abandoned as a primary discipline in our art schools. The appointment of Tracy Emin as Professor of Drawing in the Royal Academy Schools, England's oldest art school, may be a trivial event. It is nevertheless indicative of how the long history of drawing is now forgotten, or willfully misunderstood.

In saying these things, I am not advocating a return to an art based on academic drawing. Far from it. The tree of art has grown tall and its branches have spread wide. It has borne very varied fruit and can shelter great diversity beneath its shade.

Nevertheless, the taproot that ultimately nourishes all this is the visual. The eye is queen of the senses; art is her kingdom and drawing her handmaid, epitome of the relationship between eye, hand and mind on which art and its whole value to us depends. To abandon drawing is to cut that taproot. Emin's drawings though expressive show little more skill than can be found on any lavatory wall. Her appointment to such an office in an institution where drawing has been taught for nigh on two and a half centuries is symbolic of the triumph of the non-visual in the once-visual arts.

But surely art history teaches us a kind of historical determinism; that each generation gets the art it needs and deserves? There is certainly some truth in that. The rise of Brit Art, of which Emin was a leading light, coincided closely with the deregulation of the financial markets, the Big Bang as it was called. This rapidly released a flood of loose money in London. Silly money needs silly art. Canny dealers saw the opportunity and moved quickly to help soak up this new wealth. The new art market also coincided with, or was indeed a function of the neo-liberal marketisation of everything else. However, buying into the Brit Art market, into works like Damien Hirst's shark or Tracy Emin's bed and their spinoffs, this class of newly rich people were not really buying art at all, just a titillating slice of marketed notoriety.

Nevertheless, if art were exclusively shaped by such historical circumstances, if it really were predetermined, rebellion would be futile and this exhibition would have no point. But rebellion

The Curator (detail)

is not futile. It is essential. In the nineteenth century, there was a disconnect between the art that was lauded by the establishment on the one hand and the purpose of visual enlightenment which serious artists understood had shaped the art which they professed on the other. The Impressionists, the last century's most celebrated rebels, rejected the aesthetics of an age in which artists were paid more than ever before for art that was worse than ever before.

Déjà vu? Surely we are back there again? Just like the late Victorians, the present establishment has successfully hijacked the serious business of art, then as now, to use it to provide commercially marketed status symbols for the wealthy. Consequently we once again witness artists being paid colossal sums for art that is, to coin an oxymoron, quite exceptionally mediocre.

Tracy Emin, Damien Hirst and Jeff Koons are among the principal targets of Peter Goodfellow's ire and quite rightly too. It is the two latter in particular who have unashamedly embraced the commodification of art. Hirst however is closer to home although for all its self-importance, or perhaps because of it, the London art world of which he is part is also remarkably provincial. You could compare its stars to Alma Tadema, or Lord Leighton, Victorian masters of the rhetorical commodity whose reputations barely crossed the Channel.

These remarks are not just intended to make a coconut shy of established reputations. There is a serious point here about the nature and purpose of art, about judgment and our ability to make good choices. Right at the beginning of the Scottish Enlightenment, with a book called *An Inquiry into the Original of Our Ideas of Beauty and Virtue*, Francis Hutcheson launched the great philosophical arguments that were taken forward by David Hume, Adam Smith and others. Essentially Hutcheson's argument was that because they are based in feeling, not reason, our ideas of beauty, and thus our judgments in art,

are directly akin to moral judgments which he argued were equally shaped by feeling, not reason: crucially it follows, cultivation of the one will improve us in the other. Adam Smith went on to argue that the very existence of society depends on feeling, on our capacity for sympathy and sympathy in turn depends on imagination. It follows, therefore, that art as a vehicle for the cultivation of imaginative judgment also has a moral role; it should then be doubly important in our present age to help keep alive our capacity for real choice when that is being relentlessly eroded by the commercialisation of everything; when our choices are conditioned for us by ceaseless propaganda in which truth itself is merely another commodity, of greater or lesser value according to the market at the time. Sadly, too, the same can be said about our politics where marketing has supplanted ideology and truth likewise has become negotiable.

If therefore our real values are neglected and go unexamined in this way, this is no time for art to surrender its independence. These issues are its territory. Indeed it was the conviction that imagination is the faculty on which morality depends that powered modern art. The ideas that shaped it in all its many and diverse forms, the value of imagination itself, of spontaneity and expression, of originality, the admiration of the primitive, even the desire to shock, all grew from that same conviction: the social and moral value of the unfettered imagination and the consequent imperative to cultivate it and claim its freedom, unburdened by convention.

As compacted ground must be broken up to plant new seeds, so convention and the complacency it fosters, the enemies of imagination, must be disrupted. Shock has a moral value, but not dead sharks. There, modern art has abandoned its responsibility to lead and instead runs with the herd. Hirst's shark, (*The Physical Impossibility of Death in the Mind of Someone Living*), and dead cow (*Mother and Child (Divided)*) are not some poetic metaphor for any delusions of immortality

we may still retain in this post-Christian era, although they have been described as such. In our market dominated world where everything has a price, they simply represent the general commodification of the ideas that drove modern art and in particular the marketability even of the power of art to shock. When that happens, the imagination is neutered. Chained to markets and money, it is rendered impotent. Not only can it no longer disrupt the prevailing complacency. It is shackled to it. The phrase 'avant-garde' becomes meaningless, just another advertising slogan.

More cynically still, Hirst's mechanically produced paintings stand for art itself, and in particular painting, as a commodity which, like any product, can be standardised for better manu-

facture and marketing. Koons also runs a factory and his art too is a product which does not challenge, but endorses prevailing norms in order to profit from them. Indeed he remarked recently, 'I find beauty in the acceptance of cultural history,' . . . in cup cakes and Barbie dolls, perhaps? When we have sunk that low, how far have we betrayed the empirical vision of the Enlightenment philosophers and the imaginative adventures of the artists who followed them?

Hirst, Koons and Emin stand here as representatives of what has gone wrong and where the rot set in, but at the same time they and their contemporaries are also already history. It is 25 years and more since the Brit Art PR bandwagon started to roll. It was pushed along by Charles Saatchi's money. (Indeed the

Top Dog (detail)

early alliance between Saatchi, the advertising magnate, and Hirst, the artist, was indicative of the way in which the values of art and commerce were to be elided), but our art institutions also enthusiastically joined in.

Much has changed since that time, although certainly not for the better, and two things in particular have evolved to dominate contemporary art. The first is the rise to unchallenged supremacy of the Turner Prize. Cannily from the start its organisers made an alliance with television. Thus the competition has media presence; nothing matters more in the arts than that kind of visibility and it has been used relentlessly to project a narrow and tendentious view of contemporary art. Indeed the pernicious and malign influence of the Turner Prize has come to dominate contemporary art to the exclusion of all else.

Unless it is the work of an artist so close to the London establishment that they cannot be ignored, the Prize committee rigorously excludes anything that resembles conventional painting and sculpture, or to go back to where I started, any art that depends on drawing, or even on the simply visual. Indeed as Peter Goodfellow suggests in his figure of the Thought Policeman in a bubble wrap suit with a Tate bag on his head, the Turner Prize and the Tate that promotes it have spawned a thought police; and it is the curators who are these new policemen. Endorsing each other as professionals always will, they only promote art that is of the approved kind. (Indeed one major contemporary venue recently turned down a proposal to show paintings because they were the wrong kind of art and not consistent with its image.) This has created an orthodoxy, a collective opinion that is really just a crowd mentality. It is groundless as any gossip, but no voice can be raised against it.

One consequence of this unhappy situation is that there is an unbridgeable gulf in the art world between, on the one hand, self-styled contemporary art and its so dominant promoters and on the other, the art that ordinarily interested people might want to see and even buy. It is not that there is no good art being produced that could be admired. On the contrary, there are first class contemporary artists, not just painters and sculptors, but working in all sorts of unconventional ways, whose work will certainly be remembered. Go round the art school degree shows, too, and they overflow with talent exploit ing many different media. Significantly, too, when you do go round, you frequently see young artists trying to find their own way back to drawing by whatever route they can contrive. The real problem therefore is not the supply of talent, but the choice of art that gets promoted and indeed purchased, often for vast sums by our leading institutions. Its range is very narrow, as the annual Turner Prize selection makes clear, and is generally limited to certain sorts of installation and (usually lamentable) film-making.

At a time when we seem to have no firm basis on which to make judgments in art, nor indeed often even to have anything very tangible in front of us to judge, we seem to have delegated the task to the new thought police, to the contemporary art curators. Increasingly too, words, the curator's medium, though usually in an almost meaningless language that has evolved with the rise of the profession, have displaced art. In contemporary exhibitions, ubiquitous labels that tell you what to think and feel are written in a language of impenetrable, hermetic jargon. If you can deduce any sense at all from it, it usually seems to offer a wildly optimistic account of what you are actually seeing and to attribute meaning and significance to whatever sad assemblage is in front of you far beyond what it can actually support. Think of the rubbish assemblies of Turner Prize nominee Cathy Wilkes, for instance, or the unwatchable films of Luke Fowler, also a Turner Prize nominee. Hyperbolic labels appear to attribute apparently boundless ambition to mediocre works like these.

Critical judgment is lost in this dark wood of jargon. What David Levine and Alix Rule have christened IAE, International

Art English, this new language is also sinister. Like all hermetic languages, it is about the exclusion of those who are not initiates. This is particularly ironic in an age when inclusion is supposed to be the dominant ambition of our art institutions; when in pursuit of inclusion there is something very like a pop concert happening in Tate Modern and a comedian is performing in the National Gallery of Scotland. But these things are just window dressing. Exclusion is the real ambition and it is as always about power. 'IAE serves interests,' says Alix Rule. 'However laughable the language may seem to outsiders, to art-world people, speaking or writing in IAE can be a potent signal of insider status.' If you want to get on in contemporary art, you must talk and write a very special sort of nonsense.

Inevitably, too, I am afraid, you see this language in the statements art students have to write to support their work when they are being assessed. It is certainly possible that the ominously similar sounding RAE (Research Assessment Exercise), the form of assessment for funding formulated for Higher Education in the sciences that over the last couple of decades has also been forced upon the art schools, has pushed both teachers and students towards the verbal and away from the visual. When language is opaque, however, thought cannot be lucid; everything takes place in a miasma. Abuse of language muddles minds, but that also makes it easier to control them, the Thought Police again. But this verbal miasma is also the very opposite of the force and clarity of which the visual is uniquely capable; and that takes us full circle, back again to drawing and the visual disciplines on which real art is built.

Duncan Macmillan

Turner Prize Greatest Hits · oil on linen · 120 x 240 cm

debase decadent
deception decompose
deplorable deteriorate
detrimental devoid
dictatorial diminish dire
disingenuous dogma
doublespeak dubious

Top Dog · oil on linen · 61 x 92 cm

egocentric **elitism**
empty ephemera
evasion exacerbate
exaggerate exalted
excess exclude excuse
exorbitant expedient
exposure

The Client · oil on linen · 54 x 54 cm

facile factitious fallacy
farce fatuous favoured
fawn fixation flatter flimsy
folly forgettable frivolous

Omen · oil on gesso panel · 76 x 50 cm

gall garbage

gatecrash genuflect

gimmick golden-goose

grandstanding grasping

greed grotesqueries guilty

hackneyed · hamper · hanger-on
hard-sell · hauteur · hedonism
hegemony · heresy · hero-worship
hierarchy · hipster · hogwash
hoodwink · hubris · hustler
hype · hypocrisy

Omen II · oil on gesso panel · 92 x 61 cm

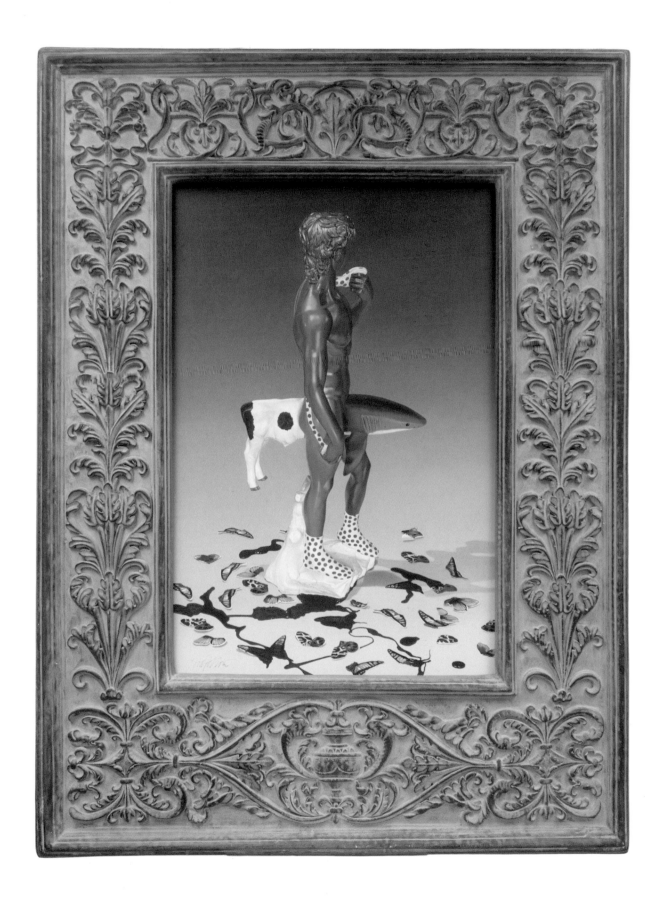

idolise immunity
impervious impose
impoverish impunity
in-crowd indefensible
indulgence infiltrate
insider intimidate
invidious irrational

JARGON

JESTER

JETSAM

JETTISON

JIGGERY-POKERY

JOBBERY

JUMBLE

JUNKET

Wallpaper · ink and collage · 26 x 35 cm

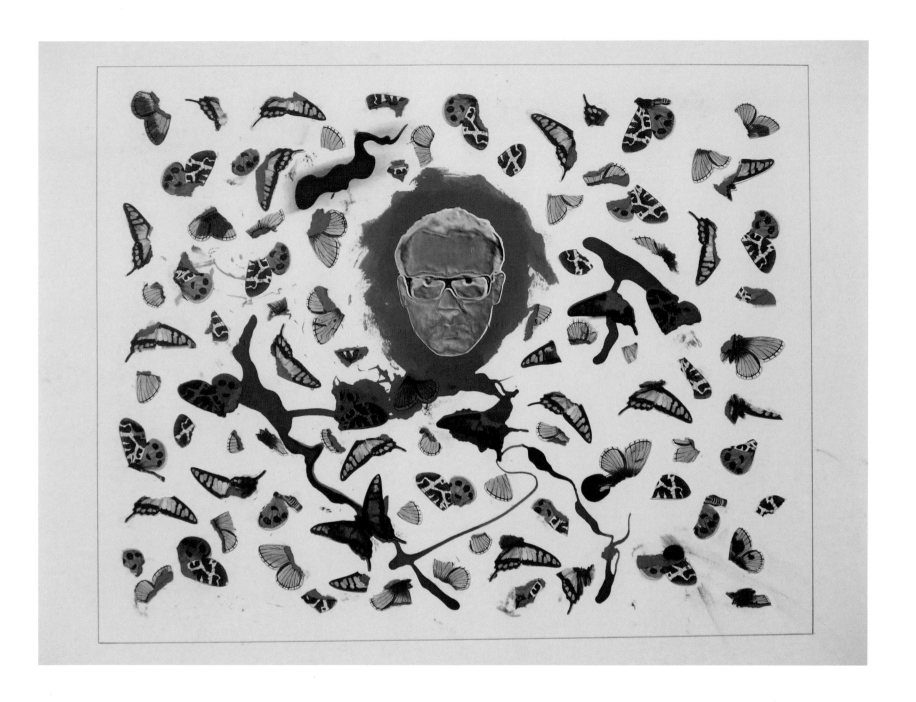

FAKING IT POINT OF VIEW · 1

'To thine own self be true,' says Shakespeare's Polonius, and thou canst be false to no man'. Live in truth, urged Václav Havel. 'Let the lie come into the world,' wrote Solzhenitsyn, 'but not through me.' How seriously should we take these pronouncements, and how do we obey them?

There are two kinds of untruth: lying and faking. The person who is lying says what he does not believe. The person who is faking says what he believes, though only for the time being and for the purpose in hand.

Anyone can lie. It suffices to say something with the intention to deceive. Faking, however, is an achievement. To fake things you have to take people in, yourself included. The liar can pretend to be shocked when his lies are exposed: but his pretence is part of the lie. The fake really is shocked when he is exposed, since he had created around himself a community of trust, of which he himself was a member.

In all ages people have lied in order to escape the consequences of their actions, and the first step in moral education is to teach children not to tell fibs. But faking is a cultural phenomenon, more prominent in some periods than in others. There is very little faking in the society described by Homer, for example, or in that described by Chaucer. By the time of Shakespeare, however, poets and playwrights are beginning to take a strong interest in this new human type.

In Shakespeare's *King Lear* the wicked sisters Goneril and Regan belong to a world of fake emotion, persuading them-selves and their father that they feel the deepest love, when in fact they are entirely heartless. But they don't really know themselves to be heartless: if they did, they could not behave so brazenly. The tragedy of King Lear begins when the real people –Kent, Cordelia, Edgar, Gloucester–are driven out by the fakes.

The fake is a person who has rebuilt himself, with a view to occupying another social position than the one that would be natural to him. Such is Molière's Tartuffe, the religious imposter who takes control of a household through a display of scheming piety, and who gave his name to the vice that his creator was perhaps the first to pinpoint with total accuracy. Like Shakespeare, Molière perceived that faking goes to the very heart of the person engaged in it. Tartuffe is not simply a hypocrite, who pretends to ideals that he does not believe in. He is a fabricated person, who believes in his own ideals since he is just as illusory as they are.

Tartuffe's faking was a matter of sanctimonious religion. With the decline of religion during the 19th century there came about a new kind of faking. The romantic poets and painters turned their backs on religion and sought salvation through art. They believed in the genius of the artist, endowed with a special capacity to transcend the human condition in creative ways, breaking all the rules in order to achieve a new order of experience. Art became an avenue to the transcendental, the gateway to a higher kind of knowledge.

Originality therefore became the test that distinguishes true from fake art. It is hard to say in general terms what originality consists in, but we have examples enough: Titian, Beethoven, Goethe, Baudelaire. But those examples teach us that originality

Turner Prize (detail)

is hard: it cannot be snatched from the air, even if there are those natural prodigies like Rimbaud and Mozart who seem to do just that. Originality requires learning, hard work, the mastery of a medium and–most of all–the refined sensibility and openness to experience that have suffering and solitude as their normal cost.

To gain the status of an original artist is therefore not easy. But in a society where art is revered as the highest cultural achievement, the rewards are enormous. Hence there is a motive to fake it. Artists and critics get together in order to take themselves in, the artists posing as the originators of astonishing breakthroughs, the critics posing as the penetrating judges of the true avant-garde.

In this way Duchamp's famous urinal became a kind of paradigm for modern artists. This is how it is done, the critics said. Take an idea, put it on display, call it art and brazen it out. The trick was repeated with Andy Warhol's Brillo boxes, and then later with the pickled sharks and cows of Damien Hirst. In each case the critics have gathered like clucking hens around the new and inscrutable egg, and the fake is projected to the public with all the apparatus required for its acceptance as the real thing. So powerful is the impetus towards the collective fake that it is now rare to be a finalist for the Turner Prize without producing some object or event that shows itself to be art only because nobody would conceivably think it to be so until the critics have said that it is.

Original gestures of the kind introduced by Duchamp cannot really be repeated–like jokes they can be made only once. Hence the cult of originality very quickly leads to repetition. The habit of faking becomes so deeply engrained that no judgement is certain, except the judgement that this before us is the 'real thing' and not a fake at all, which in turn is a fake judgement. All that we know, in the end, is that anything is art, because nothing is.

It is worth asking ourselves why the cult of fake originality has such a powerful appeal to our cultural institutions, so that no museum or art gallery, and no publicly funded concert hall, can really afford not to take it seriously. The early modernists–Stravinsky and Schoenberg in music, Eliot and Pound in poetry, Matisse in painting and Loos in architecture–were united in the belief that popular taste had become corrupted, that sentimentality, banality and kitsch had invaded the various spheres of art and eclipsed their messages. Tonal harmonies had been corrupted by popular music, figurative painting had been trumped by photography; rhyme and meter had become the stuff of Christmas cards, and the stories had been too often told. Everything out there, in the world of naive and unthinking people, was kitsch.

Modernism was the attempt to rescue the sincere, the truthful, the arduously achieved, from the plague of fake emotion. No one can doubt that the early modernists succeeded in this enterprise, endowing us with works of art that keep the human spirit alive in the new circumstances of modernity, and which establish continuity with the great traditions of our culture. But modernism gave way to routines of fakery: the arduous task of maintaining the tradition proved less attractive than the cheap ways of rejecting it. Instead of Picasso's lifelong study, to present the modern woman's face in a modern idiom, you could just do what Duchamp did, and paint a moustache on the *Mona Lisa*.

The interesting fact, however, is that the habit of faking it has arisen from the fear of fakes. Modernist art was a reaction against fake emotion, and the comforting clichés of popular culture. The intention was to sweep away the pseudo-art that cushions us with sentimental lies and to put reality, the reality of modern life, with which real art alone can come to terms, in the place of it. Hence for a long time now it has been assumed that there can be no authentic creation in the sphere of high art which is not in some way a 'challenge' to the complacencies of our public culture. Art must give offence, stepping out of the future fully armed against the bourgeois taste for the conforming and the comfortable, which are simply other names for kitsch and cliché. But the result of this is that offence becomes a cliché. If the public has become so immune to shock that only a dead shark in formaldehyde will awaken a brief spasm of outrage, then the artist must produce a dead shark in formaldehyde–this, at least, is an authentic gesture.

There therefore grew around the modernists a class of critics and impresarios, who offered to explain just why it is not a waste of your time to stare at a pile of bricks, to sit quietly through ten minutes of excruciating noise, or to study a cruci-fix pickled in urine. The experts began to promote the incom-prehensible and the outrageous as a matter of course, lest the public should regard its services as redundant. To convince themselves that they are true progressives, who ride in the vanguard of history, the new impresarios surround themselves with others of their kind, promoting them to all committees that are relevant to their status, and expecting to be promoted in their turn. Thus arose the modernist establishment–the self-contained circle of critics who form the backbone of our official and semi-official cultural institutions and who trade in 'originality', 'transgression' and 'breaking new paths'. Those are the routine terms issued by the arts council bureau-crats and the museum establishment, whenever they want to spend public money on something that they would never dream of having in their living room. But these terms are clichés, as are the things they are used to praise. Hence the flight from cliché ends in cliché, and the attempt to be genu-ine ends in fake.

What should be our response to this? If the reaction against fake emotion leads to fake art, how do we discover the real thing?

Roger Scruton

Rhine Maidens (detail)

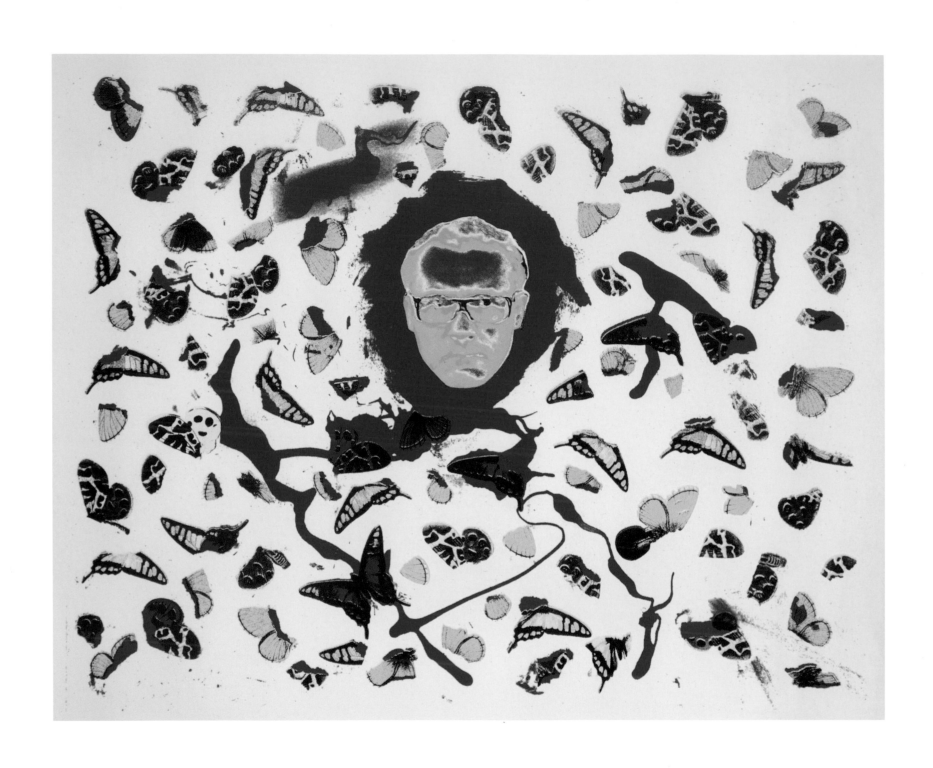

Wallpaper Acid · silkscreen (edition of 10) · 42 x 52 cm

Wallpaper Raspberry · silkscreen (edition of 10) · 42 x 52 cm

kickback
kitsch
knave
kow-tow

lackey lacklustre lamentable
laughable lessen levity
limelight **lionize** lotus-eater
lucrative ludicrous

Omen III · oil on gesso panel · 55 x 40 cm

machiavellian mafia
manipulate masquerading
meaningless mediocrity
mercenary mistaken modish
monopolise monotonous
mountebank

Omen Resurrection · mixed media · 75 x 48 x 16 cm

73

nadir
narcissism
nauseous
nescient
newspeak
nobble
nondescript
nonsense
nothing

The Rebirth of Venus · mixed media · 85 x 42 x 13 cm

obeisance obfuscate
objectionable obloquy
obscurantism obsequious
obstruct omnipotent opacity
opportunistic orwellian
ostentatious overhyped
overrated overvalued

Cup Cake Olga · oil on linen · 46 x 41 cm

Cup Cake Assunção
oil on linen · 46 x 41 cm

Cup Cake Juanita
oil on linen · 46 x 41 cm

pander pantomime
parody partisan
patronage perfidious
perishable pernicious
perpetrate pervasive
phoney platitude
plutocracy pompous
pontificate

The Two Empty Vessels · oil on canvas · 120 x 150 cm

MC AND MC

QUERCUS
ET
QUACKS
PROHIBITUM

TESORI DEL
RINASCIMENTO
ITALIANA

poseur practice

prankster predictable

preen preferential

prejudice premeditate

pretentious prima-donna

promulgate propaganda

proscribed pseudo

puerile puppet

Cup Cake Yoko · oil on linen · 46 x 41 cm

quango
quash
quisling
quotas

Wallpaper · multiple silkscreen (edition of 4) · 85 x 105 cm

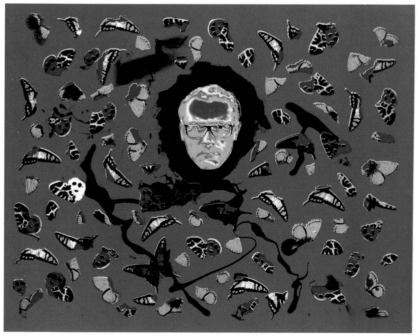
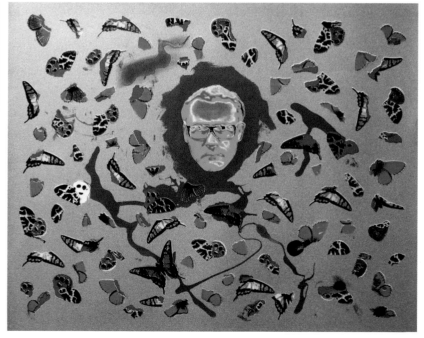

In the early years of the 20th century the arts entered a period of revolution. Enough of the escapism, the modernists said; art must show modern life as it is. Only in that way can it offer real consolation. Ornament is crime, declared the architect Adolf Loos, and all those baroque façades that line the streets of Vienna, encrusted with meaningless knobs and curlicues, are so many denials of the world in which we live. They tell us that beauty belongs in a vanished past. In the face of this message Loos set out to discover a purer beauty–beauty that belongs to modern life and also endorses it.

Loos's contemporary Arnold Schoenberg rebelled against the late romantic music of which he was such a master, saying that tonal music had become banal, and that writing in the old way led to musical clichés. Schoenberg proceeded to reinvent the language of music, hoping to recover the purity and precision of Mozart or Bach. Eliot and Pound rebelled against the fairy-tale poetry of Housman and Walter de la Mare. The task of the poet, they insisted, was not to provide nostalgic dreams but to wake us up to reality. True poetry shows things as they are, and the poet's frame of reference must be re-built in order to make this possible. The result will not be easy to understand. But, unlike the escapist poetry of the Victorians, it will be worth understanding.

In the attacks on the old ways of doing things one word in particular came into currency. That word was 'kitsch'. Once introduced the word stuck. Whatever you do, it must not be kitsch. This became the first precept of the modernist artist in every medium. In a famous essay published in 1939, the American critic Clement Greenberg told his readers that

there are only two possibilities available to the artist now. Either you belong to the avant-garde, challenging the old ways of figurative painting; or you produce kitsch. And the fear of kitsch is one reason for the compulsory offensiveness of so much art produced today. It doesn't matter that your work is obscene, shocking, disturbing–as long as it isn't kitsch.

Nobody quite knows where the word 'kitsch' came from, though it was current in Germany and Austria at the end of the 19th century. Nobody knows quite how to define the word either. But we all recognize kitsch when we come across it. The Barbie doll; Walt Disney's *Bambi*; Santa Claus in the supermarket; Bing Crosby singing *White Christmas*; pictures of poodles with ribbons in their hair. At Christmas we are surrounded by kitsch–worn out clichés, which have lost their innocence without achieving wisdom. Children who believe in Santa Claus invest real emotions in a fiction. We who have ceased to believe have only fake emotions to offer. But the faking is pleasant; it feels good to pretend; and when we all join in it is almost as though we were not pretending at all. The Czech novelist Milan Kundera made a famous observation. 'Kitsch,' he wrote, 'causes two tears to flow in quick succession. The first tear says: How nice to see children running on the grass! The second tear says: how nice to be moved, together with all mankind, by children running on the grass!' Kitsch, in other words, is not about the thing observed but about the observer. It does not invite you to feel moved by the doll you are dressing so tenderly, but by yourself dressing the doll. All sentimentality is like this: it redirects emotion from the object to the subject, so as to create a fantasy of emotion without the real cost of feeling it. The kitsch object encourages

Madonna of the Kitsch (detail)

you to think 'look at me feeling this; how nice I am and how lovable'. That is why Oscar Wilde, referring to one of Dickens's most sickly death-scenes, said that 'a man must have a heart of stone not to laugh at the death of Little Nell'.

And that, briefly, is why the modernists had such a horror of kitsch. Art, they believed, had, during the course of the 19th century, lost the ability to distinguish precise and real emotion from its vague and self-satisfied substitute. In figurative painting, in tonal music, in the cliché-ridden poems of heroic love and mythic glory, we find the same disease–the artist is not exploring the human heart but creating a puffed-up substitute, and then putting it on sale.

Of course, you can use the old styles; but you cannot seriously mean them. And if you use them nevertheless, the result will be kitsch–standard, cut-price goods, produced without effort and consumed without thought. Figurative painting becomes the stuff of Christmas cards, music becomes spineless and sentimental, and literature collapses into cliché. Kitsch is fake art, expressing fake emotions, whose purpose is to deceive the consumer into thinking he feels something deep and serious, when in fact he feels nothing at all.

However, to avoid kitsch is not so easy as it looks. You could try being outrageously avant-garde, doing something that no one would have thought of doing and calling it art; perhaps trampling on some cherished ideal or religious feeling. But, as I argued previously, this way also leads to fakes–fake originality, fake significance, and a new kind of cliché, as in so much Young British Art. You can pose as a modernist, but that won't necessarily lead you to achieve what Eliot, Schoenberg or Matisse achieved, which is to touch the modern heart in its deepest regions. Modernism is difficult; it requires competence in an artistic tradition, and the art of departing from tradition in order to say something new.

This is one reason for the emergence of a wholly new artistic enterprise, which I call 'pre-emptive kitsch.' Modernist severity is both difficult and unpopular; so artists began not to shun kitsch but to embrace it, in the manner of Andy Warhol, Allen Jones and Jeff Koons. The worst thing is to be unwittingly guilty of producing kitsch; far better to produce kitsch deliberately, for then it is not kitsch at all but a kind of sophisticated parody. Pre-emptive kitsch sets quotation marks around actual kitsch, and hopes thereby to save its artistic credentials. Take a porcelain statue of Michael Jackson cuddling his pet chimpanzee Bubbles, add cheesy colours and a layer of varnish; set the figures up in the posture of a Madonna and child; endow them with soppy expressions as though challenging the spectator to vomit, and the result is such kitsch that it cannot possibly be kitsch. Jeff Koons must mean something else, we think, something deep and serious that we have missed. Perhaps this work of art is really a comment on kitsch, so that by being explicitly kitsch it becomes meta-kitsch, so to speak.

Or take Allen Jones, whose art, recently on display at the Royal Academy, consists of female lookalikes contorted into furniture, dolls with their sexual parts made explicit by underwear, vulgar and childishly nasty visions of the human female, the whole as frothy with fake sentiment as any simpering fashion model. Again the result is such obvious kitsch that it cannot be kitsch. The artist must be telling us something about ourselves–about our desires and lusts–and forcing us to confront the fact that we like kitsch, while he pours scorn on kitsch by laying it on with a trowel. In place of our imagined ideals in gilded frames, he offers real junk in quotation marks.

Pre-emptive kitsch is the first link in a chain. The artist pretends to take himself seriously, the critics pretend to judge his product and the modernist establishment pretends to promote it. At the end of all this pretence, someone who cannot perceive the difference between the real thing and the fake decides that he should buy it. Only at this point does the chain of pretence

come to an end, and the real value of this kind of art reveal itself–namely its money value. Even at this point, however, the pretence is important. The purchaser must still believe that what he buys is real art, and therefore intrinsically valuable, a bargain at any price. Otherwise the price would reflect the obvious fact that anybody–even the purchaser–could have faked such a product. The essence of fakes is that they are not really themselves, but substitutes for themselves. Like objects seen in parallel mirrors they repeat themselves ad infinitum, and at each repetition the price goes up a notch, to the point

where a balloon dog by Jeff Koons, which every child could conceive and many could manufacture, fetches the highest price ever paid for a work by a living artist –except, of course, that he isn't one.

So what, then, is the real thing? How do we tell the real work of art and the fake apart, and why does it matter?

Roger Scruton

Brave New World (detail)

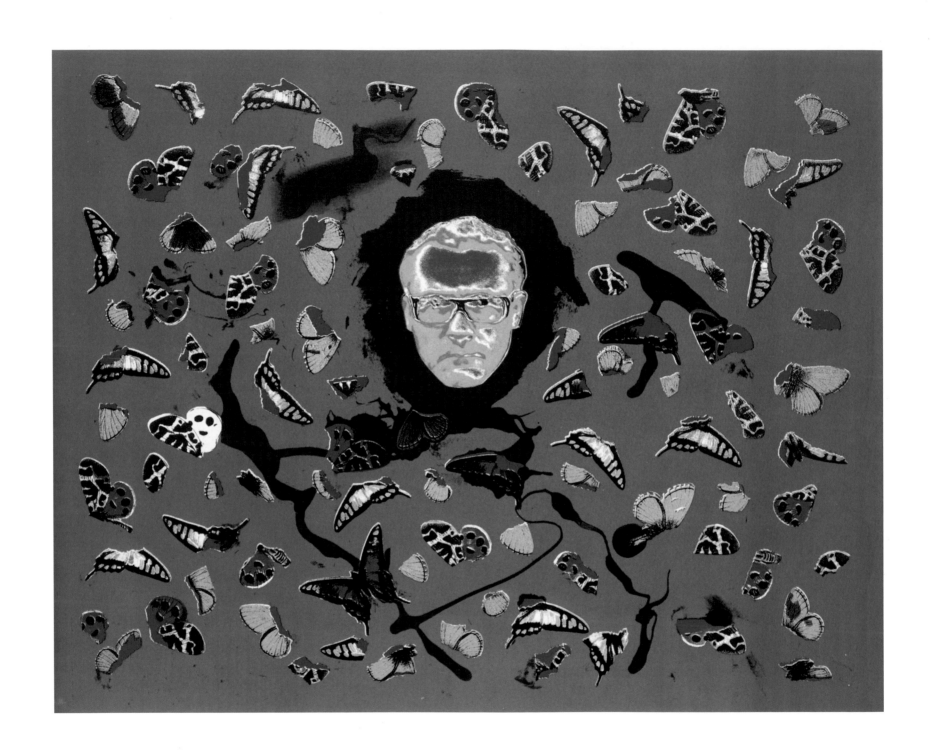

Wallpaper Cobalt · *silkscreen (edition of 10)* · 42 x 52 cm

Wallpaper Gold · silkscreen (edition of 10) · 42 x 52 cm

Madonna of the Tweet
mixed media · 51 x 27 x 8 cm

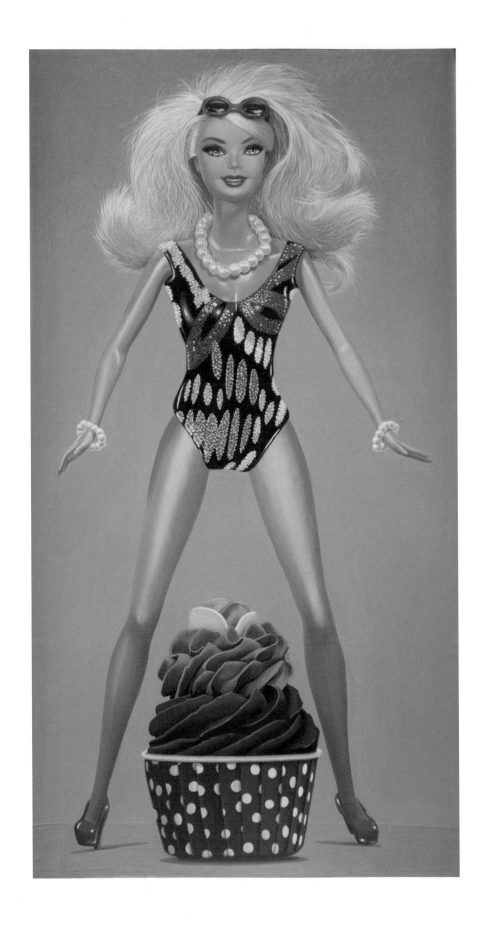

Madonna of the Cup Cake

mixed media · 51 x 27 x 8 cm

Madonna of the K9

mixed media • 51 x 27 x 8 cm

radical-chic rake-off
rapacious rebrand
reductivism regime
rehash repetition
reprehensible repress
retinue rewarded rhetoric
rigged ring-fence
ringmaster ruthless

Treason of the Sheep · mixed media · 177 x 58 cm

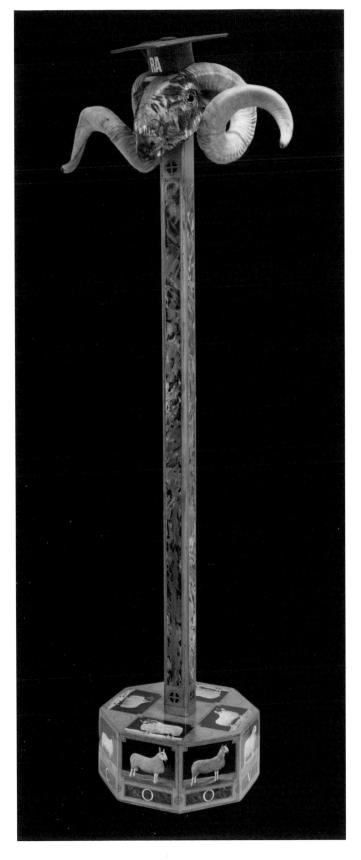

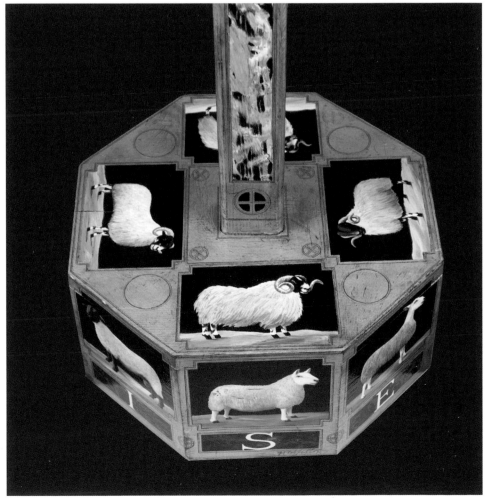

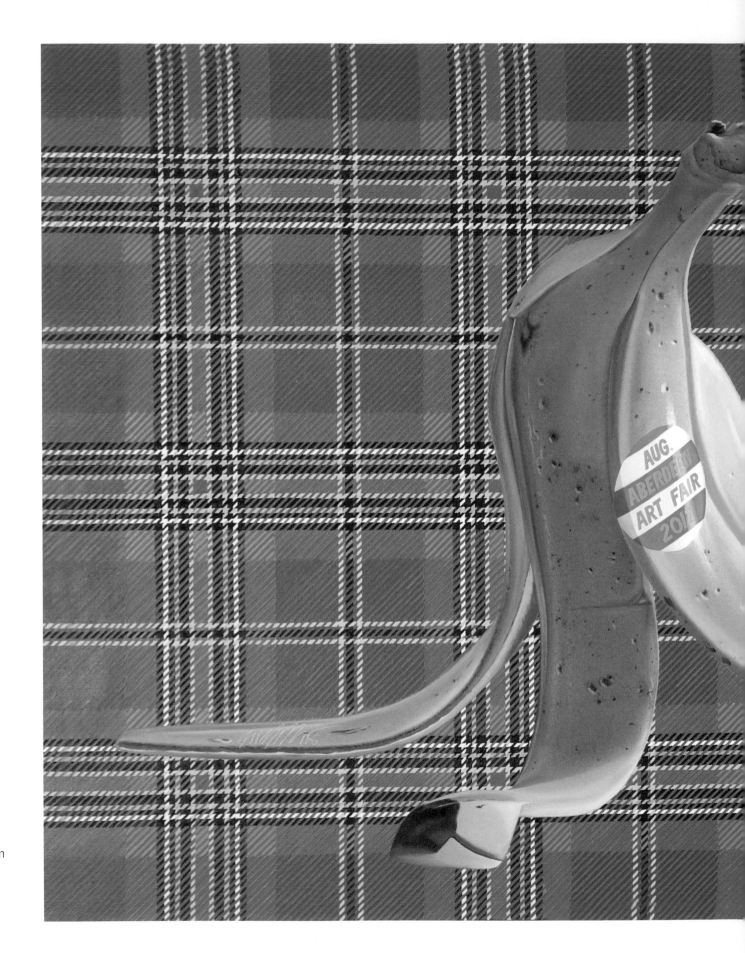

Strictly Highland

oil on canvas · 60 x 120 cm

strictly highland

sabotage sacred cow
sanctimonious sanction
sciolist self-appointed
self-conceit self-deception
self-importance self-interest
sequacious

Cup Cake Fatima · oil on linen · 46 x 41 cm

Totem Fragment · oil on linen · 100 x 135 cm

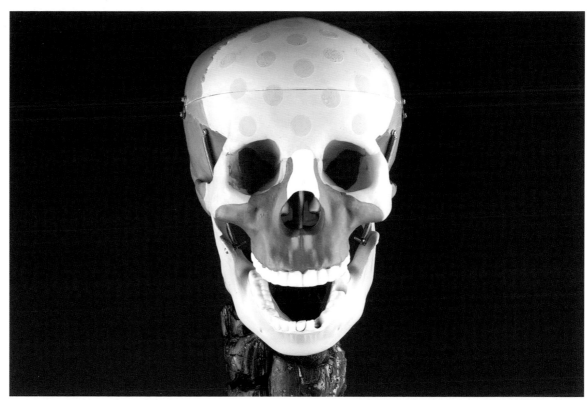
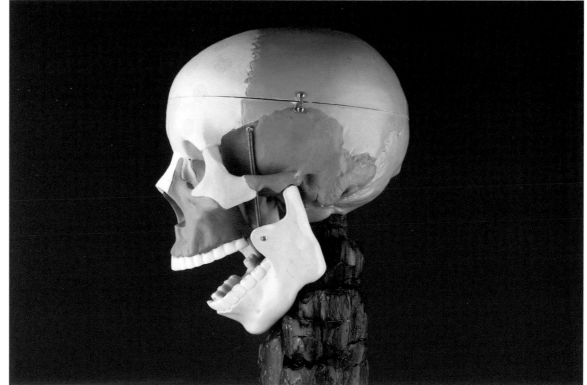

Totem of the Great Charlatan · mixed media · 190 x 36 cm

T

Rhine Maidens

mixed media · 85 x 42 x 13 cm

The III Graces
mixed media · 85 x 42 x 13 cm

The Elephant in the Room · oil on linen · 55 x 110 cm

shallow • shenanigans • shocking skulduggery

solipsism • sophistry • subsidize • succès-de-scandale

succumb • suffocate • **superficial** • surreptitious

susceptible • sycophant

Cup Cake Jamilla · oil on linen · 46 x 41 cm

tasteless tedious tendentious

thought police thrall toady tokenism

totalitarianism toxic trahison-des-clercs

travesty trendify tribal trickster

triumphalism turkey tyranny

The Curator · oil and graphite on linen · 120 x 120 cm

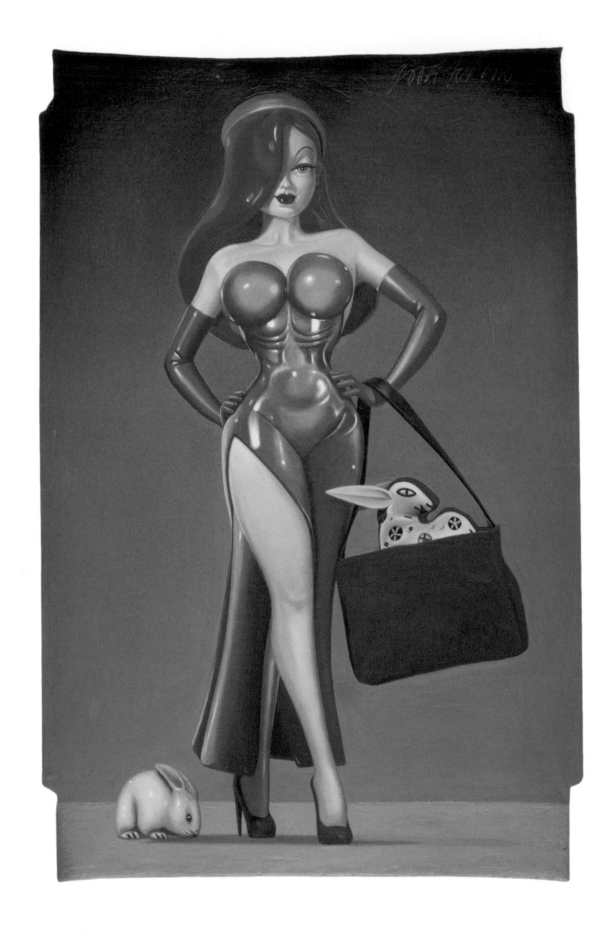

126

Mary Magdalene
mixed media · 55 x 27 x 10 cm

Mary Magdalene II
mixed media · 55 x 27 x 10 cm

unaccountable unaesthetic

unapologetic unashamed

 unassailable unchallenged

uncritical unctuous

undemocratic underhand

underwhelming undesirable

Shrine of the Prima Donna · oil on gesso panel · 42 x 53 cm

vacant vacuous vacuum

vainglory vandal vapid vassal

vaudeville venal veneer

verbiage veto virulent vogue

void voluptuary vulgar

waffle wallpaper wheeler-dealer
whimsy white-elephant whitewash
window-dressing wiseacre witless
worship worthless wrong-headed

Cabinet of Curios · oil on gesso panel · 36 x 56 cm

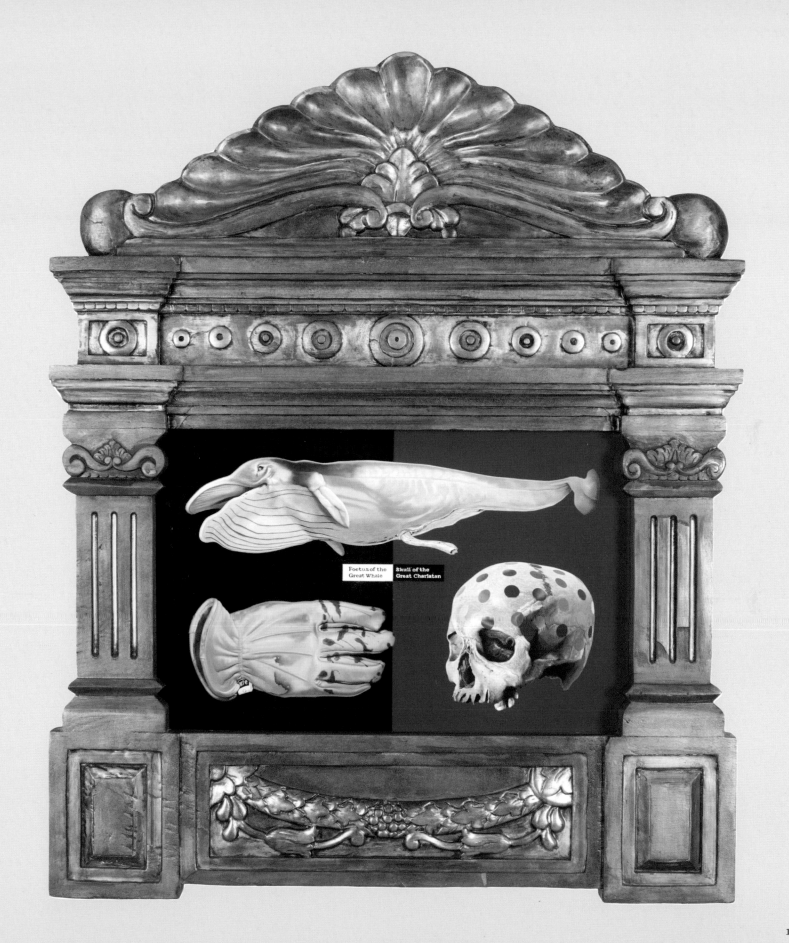

Foetus of the Great Whale

Skull of the Great Charlatan

x-rated

yawn

yes-men

yuppify

zero

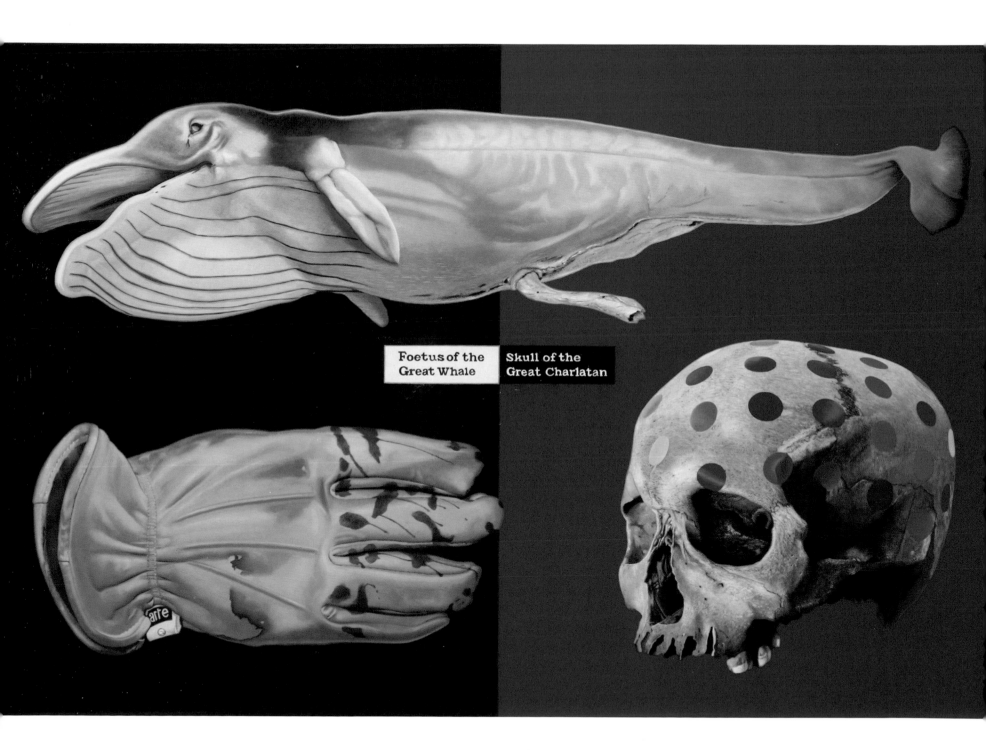

Foetus of the
Great Whale

Skull of the
Great Charlatan

The world of art, I have suggested, is full of fakes. Fake originality, fake emotion and the fake expertise of the critics–these are all around us and in such abundance that we hardly know where to look for the real thing. Or perhaps there is no real thing? Perhaps the world of art is just one vast pretence, in which we all take part since, after all, there is no real cost to it, except to those like Charles Saatchi, rich enough to splash out on junk? Perhaps anything is art if someone says that it is. Perhaps there is no such thing as a qualified judge. 'It's all a matter of taste', they say. And that's about as far as thinking goes. But is there nothing to be said in reply? Do we have no way of distinguishing true from false art, or saying why art matters and how? I shall make a few positive suggestions.

First, however, we must ignore the factors that distort our judgement. Paintings and sculptures can be owned, bought and sold. Hence there is a vast market in them, and whether or not they have a value, they certainly have a price. Oscar Wilde defined the cynic as the one who knows the price of everything, and the value of nothing. And the art market is inevitably run by cynics. Utter trash accumulates in our museums largely because it has a price tag. You cannot own a symphony or a novel in the way you can own a Damien Hirst. As a result there are far fewer fake symphonies or fake novels than there are fake works of visual art.

Things are distorted too by the channels of official patronage. The Arts Council exists to subsidize those artists, writers and musicians whose work is important. But how do bureaucrats decide that something is important? The culture tells them that a work is important if it is original, and the proof that a work is original is that the public doesn't like it. Besides, if the public did like it, why would it need a subsidy? Official patronage therefore inevitably favors works that are arcane, excruciating or meaningless over those that have real and lasting appeal.

So what is the source of that appeal, and how do we judge that a work of art possesses it? Three words summarize my answer: 'beauty', 'form' and 'redemption'.

For many artists and critics beauty is a discredited idea. It denotes the saccharine, sylvan scenes and cheesy melodies that appealed to Granny. The modernist message, that art must show life as it is, suggests to many people that, if you aim for beauty, you will end up with kitsch. This is a mistake, however. Kitsch tells you how nice you are: it offers easy feelings on the cheap. Beauty tells you to stop thinking about yourself, and to wake up to the world of others. It says, look at this, listen to this, study this–for here is something more important than you. Kitsch is a means to cheap emotion; beauty is an end in itself. We reach beauty through setting our interests aside and letting the world dawn on us. There are many ways of doing this, but art is undeniably the most important, since it presents us with the image of human life– our own life and all that life means to us–and asks us to look on it directly, not for what we can take from it but for what we can give to it. Through beauty art cleans the world of our self-obsession.

Our human need for beauty is not something that we could lack and still be fulfilled as people. It is a need arising from our

Top Dog (detail)

moral nature. We can wander through this world, alienated, resentful, full of suspicion and distrust. Or we can find our home here, coming to rest in harmony with others and with ourselves. And the experience of beauty guides us along this second path: it tells us that we are at home in the world, that the world is already ordered in our perceptions as a place fit for the lives of beings like us. That is what we see in Corot's landscapes, Cézanne's apples, or Van Gogh's unlaced boots.

This brings me to my second important word: 'form'. The true work of art is not beautiful in the way an animal, a flower or a stretch of countryside is beautiful. It is a consciously created thing, in which the human need for form triumphs over the randomness of objects. Our lives are fragmented and distracted: things start up in our feelings without finding their completion. Very little is revealed to us in such a way that its significance can be fully understood. In art, however, we create a realm of the imagination, in which each beginning finds its end, and each fragment is part of a meaningful whole. The subject of a Bach fugue seems to develop of its own accord, filling musical space and moving logically towards closure. But it is not an exercise in mathematics. Every theme in Bach is pregnant with emotion, moving with the rhythm of the listener's inner life. Bach is taking you into an imagined space, and presenting you, in that space, with the image of your own fulfilment. Likewise Rembrandt will take the flesh tints on an ageing face and show how each one captures something of the life within, so that the formal harmony of the colours conveys the completeness and unity of the person. In Rembrandt we see integrated character in a disintegrating body. And we are moved to reverence.

Formal perfection cannot be achieved without knowledge, discipline and attention to detail. People are slowly beginning to understand this. The illusion that art flows out of us, and that the only purpose of an art school is to teach us how to open the taps, is no longer believable. Gone are the days when you can make a stir by wrapping a building in polystyrene like Christo or sitting in silence at a piano for 4 minutes and 33 seconds like John Cage. To be really modern, you must create works of art that take modern life, in all its disconnectedness, and bring it to fullness and resolution, as Philip Larkin did in his great poem *The Whitsun Weddings*. It is fine for a composer to lard his pieces with dissonant sounds and cluster chords like Harrison Birtwistle; but if he knows nothing of harmony and counterpoint the result will be random noise, not music. It is fine for a painter to splash paint around like Jackson Pollock, but the real knowledge of colour comes through studying the natural world, and finding our own emotions mirrored in the secret tints of things, as Cézanne found peace and comfort in a dish of apples.

If we look at the true apostles of beauty in our time–I think of composers like Henri Dutilleux and James Macmillan, of painters like David Inshaw and John Wonnacott, of poets like Ruth Padel and Charles Tomlinson, of prose writers like Italo Calvino and Georges Perec–we are immediately struck by the immense hard work, the studious isolation, and the attention to detail which have characterised their craft. In art beauty has to be won, and the work is harder, as the surrounding idiocy grows. But the task is worth it, and this brings me to my third important word: redemption.

In the face of sorrow, imperfection and the fleetingness of our affections and joys, we ask ourselves 'why?'. We need reassurance. We look to art for the proof that life in this world is meaningful and that suffering is not the pointless thing that it so often appears to be, but the necessary part of a larger and redeeming whole. Tragedies show us the triumph of dignity over destruction and compassion over despair. In a way that will always be mysterious, they endow suffering with a formal completion and thereby restore the moral equilibrium. The tragic hero is completed through his fate; his death is a sacrifice, and this sacrifice renews the world.

Tragedy reminds us that beauty is a redemptive presence in our lives: it is the face of love, shining in the midst of desolation. We should not be surprised that many of the most beautiful works of modern art have emerged in reaction to hatred and cruelty. The poems of Akhmatova, the writings of Pasternak, the music of Shostakovich–such works shone a light in the totalitarian darkness, and showed love in the midst of destruction. Something similar could be said of Eliot's *Four Quartets*, of Britten's *War Requiem*, of Matisse's chapel at Vence.

Modernism arose because artists, writers and musicians held on to the vision of beauty, as a redemptive presence in our lives. And that is the difference between the real work of art and the fake. Real art is a work of love; fake art is a work of deception.

Roger Scruton

Brave New World (detail)

ascetic assiduous

atavistic candour

censorious clarity

classicism coherent

combative communicate

concentrate conscience

courage critical crusader

determination diligence

disaffected ethical

faculty fortitude frank

The Legacy of Joseph Beuys (Jean Goodfellow) · oil on canvas · 100 x 120 cm

heartfelt

illuminate

independent

integrity

irony

justice

lampoon

maturity

meticulous

nil-desperandum

non-conformist

northerner

observant

outsider

painstaking

passion

perfectionist

perplexed

persistent

pertinacious

polemic

principles

professional

quixotic

reason

reawaken

rebalance

rebel

rediscover

resurrect

rubicon

sardonic

satirical

scrupulous

serious

subversive

succès d'estime surgical technique

tenacious thought-provoking topical

tradition troublemaker unaffiliated

unambiguous unauthorized unconnected

undeterred unwelcome vehement

veracious whistle-blower wholehearted

wilderness wilful zeal

All Dressed Up for Mam and Dad · oil on canvas · 150 x 120 cm

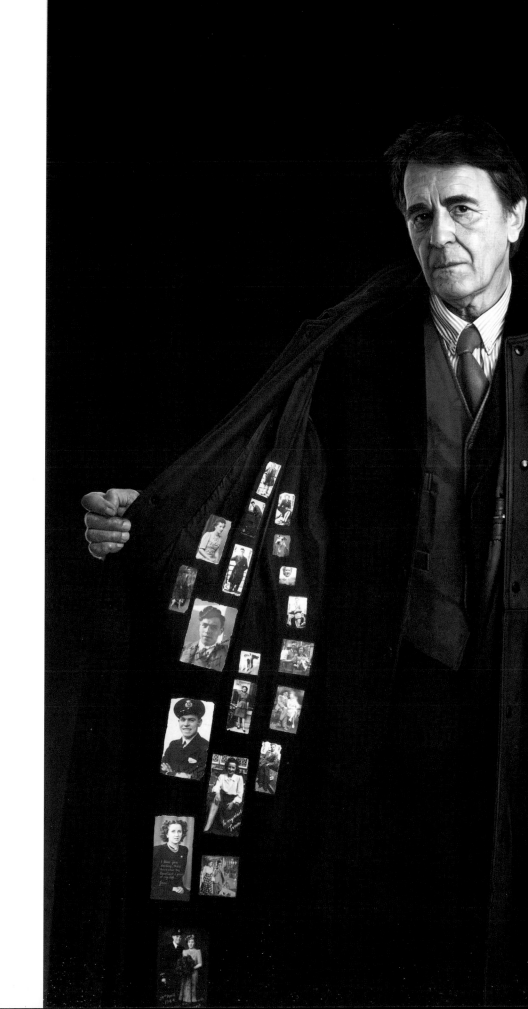

PETER GOODFELLOW

b. Middlesbrough, 1950

EDUCATION

Billingham North Primary, Bede Hall Grammar School

1967–8 Foundation course, Middlesbrough College of Art

1968–71 Degree Course, Central School of Art, London

Peter's professional career as a freelance illustrator was mainly in the field of book jacket, advertising and packaging design. With agents in New York, Hamburg and London he established himself as one of Europe's leading illustrators. In 1995 Peter switched careers and established himself as one of Scotland's foremost landscape painters. Over the last few years a new direction has emerged featuring portraits and the urban environment, and in some works a highly political content is beginning to evolve.

EXHIBITIONS

2013–15	Panter & Hall, London
2014	Mall Gallery, London
2013–15	Gallery Heinzel, Aberdeen
2013	National Portrait Gallery, Edinburgh
2012–15	Frames Gallery, Perth
2012	National Portrait Gallery, London
	Balman Gallery, Corbridge
2010	Iona House, Woodstock
2009	Geneva International Art Fair
2009–15	Red Rag Gallery, Stow on the Wold
2009–14	Tallantyre Gallery, Morpeth
2005–09	Kranenburg & Fowler, Oban
2005–07	Duff House, Banff
2004–15	Duncan Miller, London
2004–09	Tracey McNee Gallery, Glasgow
2002–14	Aberdeen Art Gallery
2002	The Biscuit Factory, Newcastle
2000–15	AAF, London
2000–10	Glasgow International Art Fair
2000	Osborne Gallery, London
	Lennox Gallery, London
1998–2012	Leith Gallery, Edinburgh
1997–2015	The Lost Gallery, Strathdon
1997–2015	Milton of Crathes, Banchory
1996	Toloquhon Gallery, Tarves
1994	Open Eye Gallery, Edinburgh; also 1996
1993	Margarethe Hubauer, Hamburg; also 1994, 97

1994	Warehouse Gallery, London
	Browns Gallery, Tain; also 1998, 2011
1993	90s Gallery, Glasgow
	The Kenny Gallery, Galway; also 1994, 96
1992	Riverside Gallery, Stonehaven; also 93, 95, 97, 98, 2009, 12
1989	Rendezvous Gallery, Aberdeen
1987	Neal Street Gallery, London
1985	Swiss International Illustration Exhibition
1984	Det Norske Veritas, Copenhagen
1981	Maddermarket, Norwich
1979	Frankfurt Book Fair; also, 1988, 1994
1979, 1984	World Science Fiction Convention, Brighton
1977	Science Fiction Publishers Convention, Oxford
1976–89	Association of Illustrators Annual Exhibition, London
1976, 1979	Victoria & Albert Museum
1975, 1979	Illustrators Gallery, London
1976–85	European Illustration, London

COMMISSION

2000–2 Commissioned by the Hon Phillip Astor to design and paint a series of art works (24) and three stained glass windows for private chapel in Migvie, Aberdeenshire

PUBLIC & COMMERCIAL COLLECTIONS

Victoria & Albert Museum
Saatchi & Saatchi
Whitbread
Penguin Books
Baxter's Foods
William Collins & Sons
Scandutch, Denmark
ICL
National Savings
British Telecom
Quantas Airline
Scania Motors, Sweden
Grisewood & Dempsey Publisher
Bergsoe, 3, Denmark
Peter Justenson, Denmark
Cidel Bank, Luxembourg
Intergrated Engineering Services, Aberdeen
BBC
Duncan & Todd, Aberdeen
CBC, Copenhagan

ACKNOWLEDGEMENTS

Points of View courtesy of the BBC and Roger Scruton

All Dressed up for Mam and Dad is reproduced with the
kind permission of Richard and Elaine Austin

SPECIAL THANKS

Philip Mould, Morgan Philips, Tiffany Panter
Mathew Hall, Jim Livingston, Craig Mackay
Claus Bruun, Philip Astor, Jamie Howse
Frank and Paul Gilfeather, . . . and especially
to my wife, Jean Goodfellow

DEFINITIONS

The Concise Oxford English Dictionary

PUBLISHED BY
PANTER & HALL LIMITED
11–12 PALL MALL, LONDON, SW1Y 5LU

COPYRIGHT ©2015 PANTER & HALL LIMITED

FRAMES AND GILDING • HUGH GORING
BESPOKE WOODWORK • DEREK STUART
BOOK DESIGN • ALAN AND MELANIE BALDWIN
TYPOGRAPHY • STRULE STEELE
PHOTOGRAPHY • PICTII
PRINT • JNVPRINT
PRINTED & BOUND IN COLCHESTER, ENGLAND

WWW.PETERGOODFELLOW.COM
WEB DESIGN • GORDON MCKNIGHT

DVD • FRANK GILFEATHER ASSOCIATES & CINÉCOSSE

BRITISH LIBRARY CATALOGUING-IN-PUBLICATION DATA
A CATALOGUE RECORD FOR THIS BOOK
IS AVAILABLE FROM THE BRITISH LIBRARY

ISBN 978-0-9933568-0-3

Venetian Red · oil on canvas · 100 x 120 cm

Venetian Fragment 2 (study) · oil on canvas · 11 x 22 cm